IT'S STILL THERE;
IT DOESN'T HURT

To Kathleen,
God Bless you,
You made a difference
with me. Thank you,

IT'S STILL THERE; IT DOESN'T HURT

Poetry about PTSD

PETER ROMPF

Palmetto
PUBLISHING GROUP

Palmetto Publishing Group
Charleston, SC

It's Still There; It Doesn't Hurt
Copyright © 2018 by Peter Rompf
All rights reserved

First Edition

Printed in the United States

ISBN-13: 978-1-64111-125-6
ISBN-10: 1-64111-125-9

Dedication

This collection of poems is dedicated to Dr. Valentina Stoycheva, who after reading several of my poems inspired me to complete my unfinished work. It was her encouragement that led to my aspiration that compelled me to copyright and publish the thoughts of my life experiences through poetry. Dr. Stoycheva in many ways held the torch to give me light when there was just darkness.

Thanks to the late Gill Rooney, God rest her soul, who in 2015 started to show me how to cope with the past and live for the future.

Thanks to Kathleen Casey and Sandra Schlesinger for their dedication to me, and so many other veterans, in their struggles to recover. They were also a tremendous factor in encouraging me to capture my reflections and propel them to the next level.

God Bless my late mother, Margaret, who exposed me to classic literature, music, and the fine arts.

Most of all, I dedicate these poems to my loving wife, Jean, who has stood by me these thirty-eight years, through my horror, confusion, and disarray. She has been the calm after the storm.

INTRODUCTION

I enlisted in the Army in 1984 and wore the uniform for thirty-three years. During the Gulf War, I was a combat engineer from A Co Twelfth Engineer Battalion, attached to Third Armored Division (Second Brigade, 3-8 Calvary) part of the VII Corps, Europe. I took part in the largest tank battle since WWII, when my unit clashed with the Iraqi Republican Guard, Tawakalna ala-Allah, tank division.

After the cease fire, Alpha Company was assigned to Safwan in southern Iraq. Our mission was to uncase, stack, and detonate ammunition left by the Republican Guard. This consisted of large ammunition dumps of 122mm rockets from Brazil. It was later identified these rockets contained saran gas, mustard gas, and biological warheads. The location was also extremely near the burning oil wells in Kuwait. The burning oil wells poured hazardous dioxins in the air, with black smoke that gave the illusion of the day looking like early evening.

The author is in the back row on the right.

After that mission, Alpha Company was assigned to refugees at Basra, in southern Iraq. At Basra, the collation used a giant cement factory to house the refugees. The children would go outside the compound and pick up unexploded ordinance. Some children lost their arms or legs. Some children lost their lives. The lifeless children became a feeding frenzy for the wild dogs at night.

From there, A Co was attached to check points along the Iraq and Saudi Arabia border. The mission was to search vehicles and personnel for firearms and ammunition. Our orders also called for separating males between eighteen and twenty-five years of age and turn them over to the military police for questioning. I will never forget the screams and tears of the parents as their sons were separated from their families.

During the Shiite uprising in southern Iraq, the Republican Guard unmercifully massacred village after village. The Shiites came to our camp at night with wagons of their dead children, asking us to please shoot them, as they no longer wanted to live. They asked us why the US did not protect them against the massacres and why we let Saddam Hussein kill their children.

These are just a few of many instances I witnessed of the crimes against humanity. Upon my return to Germany, I was physically and mentally a different person. My wife and two children started to see me slowly evolve into someone they did not know.

During the attack of the World Trade Center on September 11, 2001, I was assigned to the New York City Recruiting Battalion, Fort Hamilton Brooklyn. As the Operations NCO, I saw firsthand the towers burning and could smell the jet fuel. Fort Hamilton, which was right across the bay, was made an outpost for the Pentagon. There were bomb scares on post almost every day. Recruiting stations in Manhattan and Brooklyn were also threatened. The work hours and atmosphere were like combat conditions.

During Freedom Iraq, the recruiting missions (quotas) were of extreme pressure. Pressure to violate personal integrity, threats of promotion denial through annual evaluations, threats of family time, along with work hours of twelve to over sixteen hours per day. This led to destroyed marriages, infidelity, spousal abuse, child abuse, substance abuse, violent behavior, and suicide.

In 2015, while separated from my wife for the second or third time, it finally dawned on me that maybe, just maybe, I might have a problem. After twenty-five years, I took that big step. I was diagnosed with PTSD going all the way back to the Gulf War in 1991.

I wrote the majority of these poems from 1998 to 2004. I put them away for years, but the ghosts and reoccurring images were always with me. In 2015, I read them again, and it became obvious that many of the metaphors were about my personal struggles. Since then, I finished several poems that I had started years ago and wrote a few new ones. My poems were my inner self trying to reach out and make sense of my torments.

The Old Man's Friendship

Sinatra sings "Summer Wind."
The old man slowly walks in.
Cigarettes and dollar bills on the bar.
The shot glass and beer, his companions, are not far.
No one to go home to, no one knows he is there.

(Sinatra singing)
"And still those days,
Those lonely days
They go on and on
And guess who sighs his lullabies
To all the nights that never end?"

Looking at his glass, he sighs, "My huckleberry friend."
Customers walk by like he is not even there.
The attention he gets is when his glass is filled with air.
The newspaper is turned page by page;
the wall mirror shows his true age.
Another pupil sits on the stool,
present for the establishment's night school.
Running his fingers through his hair,
with his shaking hand, he waves the glass in the air.
A smile and a laugh come from his face;
he sits alone in this crowded place.
Looking at his empty hand, he clenches a fist.
The anger he feels, from life he has missed.
Picking up the remnants of what he had placed down.

He leaves the change; he looks around.
Downing what is left in his glass,
his acquaintance assures him their friendship will last.
He gets up and slightly staggers to the street;
the silence of the night is the only one he is destined to meet.
Stopping and leaning against a pole,
he hears the turn signal telling him he may go.
The long walk home, he can see his breath;
the acquaintance assures him, home there is friendship left.

(Sinatra singing)
"Then softer than
That piper man
One day, it called to you
And I lost you
I lost you to the summer wind"

"Summer Wind" lyrics by Hans Bradtke, Henry Mayer,
Johnny Mercer.

It's Still There; It Doesn't Hurt

Sitting here in this old oak chair
with the stain and varnish worn.
I remove my hands from the upholstered
arms, seeing how it's yellowed and torn.
I zip up my jacket to hide my white stained shirt.
It still bothers me, even though it doesn't hurt.

My morning coffee, now turned cold,
no longer a pleasure to smell or hold.
I put the cup down on the table nearby
while waiting for the phone to ring as the day goes by.

Looking at the photographs on the wall,
I notice they are crooked, faded, about to fall.
Cracks spreading on the plaster, like stepping on thin ice,
webs in the corners reaching to entangle someone's life.

Checking the time, I look at the clock;
the room is silent except for the sound
of the empty tick-tock.
I turn my head and look at the phone;
it hasn't rung; I am still all alone.

Opening the curtains to bring in more light,
staring at the sky, not blue, not bright.
Clouds so large, clouds so gray, it's almost
hard to tell it's day.

Choking the curtains, closing them with a jerk,
I stare at the phone; it smiles back with a smirk.

I look in the mirror on the door.
I see my reflection, I see it all.
I see the stain on my shirt,
the jacket still on; it doesn't hurt.

I look at my face.
I judge every imperfection.
I look deep in my eyes,
black pupils filled with rejection.
Running my fingers through my hair,
reflecting on memories good and bad.
Memories of good times gone by,
memories which refuse to die.

I pull my mind from deep space
back to the present, back to this decaying place.
Looking down at my shoes, I see the laces are broken.
I tie them together and hide the knot so it is not showing.

Waiting for the phone to ring all day,
I get up and walk away.
Down the long hall, I walk to my room,
step by step; another day will be over soon.
Turning the knob and opening the door,
still trapped in this life I've led before.
Lying down and falling asleep,
I sigh; maybe it will all change next week.

I Have Been Here Before

I have been here before;
I can feel it as I touch the wall.
The feeling of an outer-body existence,
the feeling that has only lasted an instant.
I shudder and shake my head,
as if it were electricity I was fed.
I see it in the corner of her eye;
I see it as she walks by.
I see it as she turns her head;
I see it as she says goodbye.
A message she is trying to relay.
Something happened to her one day.
Something in her voice is very soothing.
Something in her appearance
making her an illusion.
I question if she is real
or is my mind playing a cruel game.

I have been here before;
I cannot remember anymore.
As I touch the articles, they bring me near.
I try to concentrate, and the memory disappears.
I see her heading this way;
then she turns and walks away.
As if it were something I said,
as if I had an appearance she did dread.
I see it in the room that surrounds us;
I see it in the vision that has found us.

I see it, as I watch her leave.
I see it, but do I believe?
It was fourteen years today,
the day she went away.
The empty times that filled up my life,
the pain that cuts deep as a knife.
Never wanting anyone to take her place,
a constant void, like never-ending space.

I have been here before,
never endless, like mankind and war.
I cannot remember the particular reason.
But it constantly happens like the changing seasons.
I see it as she stands in front of me,
the look in her eye that haunts me.
Looking at me with a question on her face,
motioning for me to leave this place.

I have been here before;
I put the gun down and slam the drawer.
I scream, "Go away!"
This act will not happen today.
Disappointed, she states she understands.
She will always come back to lend a helping hand.
Her soothing voice, gone for today,
upset she could not take him away.
Is this real or is it an illusion?
Is it my mind in tossed confusion?
Does she appear to take me away,

back to fourteen years ago, before the dreadful day?
It is not my fault that we are alone,
unable to cross into the other's zone!
I have been here before, fourteen times, as a matter of fact,
edging me to the same ending act.
I splash cold water on my face.
This lonely life, I do not want to waste.

The Autumn Leaf

Catching the corner of my eye
Up in the turbulent sky
Yellow like the sun
Once green, its life almost done
Like a sailboat in the bay
At sunset far away
An autumn leaf all alone
Like a sailboat far from home
Its stem like a rudder cutting through the breeze
Handling life with such ease
I close my eyes and smile
I think of her; it's been a while
Opening my eyes, I see the yellow leaf is gone
Vanishing like a sailboat in the storm
I see the bare trees, branches like fingers
Reaching out to the open air
Reaching out to nowhere
The splendor of summer is gone
The bitter winter is born
I close my eyes and cry
I think of her; it's been such a long while
Looking above my head
There it is, now yellow and red
Soon to rest, soon to go
Soon buried beneath the snow
Somewhat dormant, lying on the ground
Born again like new love found

I close my eyes, and she is gone
The sun is high; the water is calm
The sailboat returns, not lost at sea
Its sails need mending, ripped and torn
The yellow leaf is gone

The Door

Standing in front of the door,
looking oddly different,
as if I have seen it before.
Placing my hand on the smooth surface,
my fingers feel and follow the grain.
A paint chip falls on the floor,
revealing a color I thought this wood never wore.
A color in contrast to the present surroundings.
A personality covered trying to break through,
shedding a different light
to something that I thought I knew.

My hand turns the worn brass knob.
The mechanism slips, the latch is still ajar.
This door has always opened for me before.
Is its hidden color trying to tell me more?
I take a step back to look and see.
It is plain and simple what has conspired to me.

I thought I knew just how you worked—
your mechanics, your swings, your every little quirk.
Looking back, it is so very clear.
My memory races, the pictures appear.
You have cried out that you need repair.
Your squeaks, your hollows, the scratches, the despair.
The very hinges that carried your weight,
the awful burden, you realize it is not too late.

The Light of the New Day

Awake at the window, unable to sleep.
The morning approaching, still dark and deep.
My exhale fogs the glass.
The warmth of the room, it does not last.
Off in the distance among the bare trees,
one evergreen I can barely see.
The dark of the night starts to disappear;
the light of the sun slowly creeps to the top of the trees.
The rays gently penetrating down,
the branches and green needles can now be found.
The evergreen needles respond to the new morning glow.
It is almost time for me to go.
The sun starts to warm the damp ground.
The vapors escape, drifting endlessly about;
they dance to the melody like a saxophone puts out.

The morning light gently brushing my face,
the morning light taking me to a new place.
I turn and see the day's new light,
still an infant, not yet in flight.
The new morning sun crawls over her face.
Like fog, it moves at a slow rolling pace.
My hand gliding with the sun,
I do not touch you, so you can sleep on.

A tear forms in the corner of my eye;
it glides down, like a child on a slide.

The thousand times we made the world stand still,
complacent, for granted, weakness and strong will.
You slowly move, as the sun feeds you life.
The moon and the stars have gone with the night.
Buried with the start of this new day,
buried behind the clouds, to play.

Walking across the field,
passing the evergreen with much appeal.
The tree's color, green all year round,
an amazing feat of nature to be endowed.
"Hello, my friend, how are you today?"
Admiring the colors of the watching blue jay.
The bird tilting his head
as if understanding the question said.

Nearing the split rail fence,
I see the ground is still moist and dense.
Kicking the collected soil gathered around my shoe,
it falls in the grass and melts with the fresh morning dew.

The blue jay landing on the windowsill,
watching her curiously, lying still.
As she felt a presence and opened her eyes,
the blue jay spread his wings to fly.

Different Directions

Daylight leaves the earth and turns to night.
The perils of darkness are filled with the morning light.
The orange sun in the morning sky
casts a prehistoric image in my mind.
Each magnificent, in their own way,
only when combined, gives us another day.
The day and night do not work in different directions
but complement each other in a daily resurrection.

Another day for the images to appear
from the mind to the heart; it's tearing me apart.
The ghosts that only I know are both shallow and deep.
Every night they invade my sleep.
The sounds and smells never to go away;
dormant in my mind, they lay.

The gravity of the moon pulls the ocean from the shore.
Yet the water always returns to embrace the wet marsh
once more.
The water stretched by a force so strong,
coexisting in natures aggression, never in different
directions.

I fight the images to vanish from my mind.
Their force is too strong; they pull me back to that time.
I relive the horror again and again.
I am presently in two worlds, now and then.

The salmon swimming against the river's current,
exhausted from the restless migration,
finds peace and tranquility, reaching their final destination.
The river current and the salmon are not forces of
different direction
but vehicles intertwining to achieve a beautiful restoration.

My soul rolling like tumbleweed to who knows where.
No direction, just despair.
I search for the lighthouse that will guide me through the
fog.
I search for the night that will turn to day.
I search for the water that returns to the marches.
I search for the salmon that conquers the river current,
that I may find tranquility, resurrection, and restoration.

The Highway of Emptiness

Fast or slow, it doesn't matter how you go.
North or south, east or west;
they all lead to the Highway of Emptiness.
All those moments lost in time
race by you like road signs.
Time heals nothing; it stays in your head.
Your soul continues to cry after you are dead.

The wild dogs and vultures in their nest
all feed off the Highway to Emptiness.
Eyes of anger, eyes of fear
litter the highway with puddles of tears.
No floods, blizzards, or earthquakes can close the road,
but there are many tolls that burden your soul.
You are a highway statistic of a different view.
You bled from the inside, nobody knew.

Happy then sad, laugh then cry, love then hate.
It stirs your brain to conflate.
Numb with no emotions, stay away.
Senseless, lethargic, indifferent, and dazed.
Your emotions, trapped in an eclipse of Aeschylus,
you have just entered the Highway of Emptiness.

Red and white but the inkblot is black and blue.
The paper is round; you haven't a clue.
The man with the tie says, "Why do you lie?

What's wrong with you?
Can't you see, it's as plain as can be!
I'll prescribe this, take two."

The stick gives a strike;
the sulfur ignites.
You hold your breath in;
the altered feeling begins.
Immobilized, benumbed, and unhinged.
Awake and compendious,
you have returned to the Highway of Emptiness.

The Reflection

The reflection of the trees on the lake's water
made me shiver as my memory began to melt.
Looking at the bones in my hand,
I see the roads to everything I felt.
The veins crossing the roads like rivers,
emptying in between the fingers.
The lines on the back of my hand zig zagging, trying to
    find where I am.
Fingernails, calm water in a lagoon.
The breeze sweeps from the ocean, temporarily cool.

My memory brings me back to a song,
a song I haven't heard for so long.
It sings about the crossroads, the freight cars, "Sweet
Melissa."
A song that can calm the rough sea,
a song that was written about someone I see.
Stars in the heaven, stars on the plains,
different worlds, they will drive you insane.
You let her go like sand running through your hand,
blending in with the ground,
gone never to be found.
My finger running upward from the neck to the chin,
a salmon on an annual swim.
Now circling the lips on my face,
the hill, the valley, it used to lead someplace.
Both hands cross over the nose.

The breath exhales, the warm wind blows.
Bowing my head and holding it in my hands,
the two become one and form a new land.
The lines, the veins, the roads, the rivers, the calm lagoon.

Leave Them All

Standing at the waterfront, staring at the fog,
I can barely see the sea; I can hear where you are.
I hold up my hand; the air is damp and cold.
I wipe off the moisture, no one with me to hold.
The waves make a crack; it sounds just like thunder.
I feel the cold water as the wave pulls me back from under.

I see the ship in the distance, far, far away.
She invites me, she seduces me, she calls me to play.
Moving in and out of the fog, like a ghost through a wall,
she cries, "Come to me, come to me, forget them all."
Her distant lights are burning bright,
with a haze of different colors.
She draws me in, like she did with so many others.
I roll my shoulders; I run my hand down my sweater.
I feel the holes; I begin to shudder.
I tell myself it's okay, but I have never felt this way.
I take a step; I move along the shore; I look at the ship.
I don't care; I want more.

I hear her call with the sound of the horn,
"Come to me, come to me, forget them all."
The ship fades in, the ship fades out,
like a white mountain peak, with clouds floating about.
She moves smooth across the calm sea,
as if she were saying, "Come along, chase me."
I stand in the water staring straight out.
The water is cold; I don't pull out.

I want to go farther, but she is too far to swim.
The anchor has just dropped; the ship won't come in.
I ask myself the question, "Am I doing the right thing?"
She is full of mystery; I don't understand what she sings.
The ship moves swiftly, moving out of sight.
The lights grow dim, blending into the night.
I turn around and look at the barren shore.
I make a decision; there is nothing here for me anymore.

I let my mind drift, like the winds over the seas.
I hear the soft voice, "Come to me;
this is where you want to be."
My soul departs on a blue flying carpet.
Within seconds, I have achieved my desired target.
As I grab the ship's railing and look at the white shore,
I see myself standing, waving as before.

It's Been Too Long

Where have all the people gone?
Ah, but it's been too long
since a man has tipped his hat to a lady,
since someone has sung a pretty song.
I used to see a movie and hear the chorus of the heavens,
smile and know there is hope at the ending.
Whatever happened to large brim hats and I beg your pardon.

Where have all the people gone?
I search for them from dusk to dawn.
I look for a sign in the atmosphere.
I look at the faces, not a chance of cheer.
They all read, "What do you have for me?"
Then reply, "Don't bother me."

Whatever happened to taking a bow?
Having a conversation with some know how?
Children calling adults by mister and ma'am,
the art of kissing a lady's hand.

Where have all the people gone?
Yes, it's been far too long.
Since I live for you, and you live for me,
this is the way the world was meant to be.
Whatever happened to pride in one's work?
Rolling up those sleeves and dirty the white shirt.
Helping others and putting them first,

seeing a black and white movie with Rita Hayworth.
The art of charm is far away;
Mrs. Emma Peel, come back and play.

Where have all the people gone?
They are back where they belong?
Take this as you may:
Are they still here, or just with yesterday?

She Escapes Reality

Thirty-nine years old and still all alone.
To escape reality, she gets stoned.
After five minutes, life is okay;
she is ready to face another day.
Brilliant at work, strong and domineering,
known as Top Gun, she has men fearing.
Standing tall with long black hair,
a business suit, and a cunning stare.
In conversation, she will win you over.
Make you laugh, a great sales closer.
Her only goal that really matters
is achieving the steps up the corporate ladder.

She thinks of him and hopes he will call;
she has to get away from it all.
Hoping that he will come by,
then playing the helpless female, in the blink of an eye.
He leaves in the morning to return in three days.
It's his wife's and children's turn;
she is told to behave.

Thirty-nine years old and still all alone.
To escape reality, she gets stoned.
After five minutes, life is okay;
she is ready to face another day.
She has just learned there are no friends at work;
coworkers are jealous, coworkers hurt.

Some try to seize the opportunity, to steal her creations.
She is too sharp, she is too clever;
another friend terminated for the better.

Wants to start a relationship with Mr. Right,
buy a condominium, sleep with him every night.
She sighs and she falls, all good men are taken.
She waits for him to call; she waits for her safe haven.
He leaves in the morning, promising the weekend.
She sees in his eyes, come Friday there will be a
cancellation.

Thirty-nine years old and still all alone.
To escape reality, she gets stoned.
After five minutes, life is okay;
she is ready to face another day.

A Beautiful Person

She moves and looks with confidence,
yet is reserved.
Feminine, but not helpless.
Beautiful eyes with a matching smile.
I think a dreamer, like myself.
She knows what she wants
but doesn't tell everything
naturally of course.
She makes me feel relaxed;
she makes me communicate my thoughts
as if she already knows—maybe she does.
Lifestyles in common, she understands my world;
I understand hers.
Thinks a lot of herself, likes to help others.
Now wants to help herself.
Doesn't try to impress, but naturally does,
a beautiful person.

Some Thoughts on Where My Life Has Gone

Look at the leaves, red, yellow, and green.
Look at the squirrels running in between.
I have never noticed how big these trees have grown.
I am glad I have finally found time, as I sit here all alone.
Why haven't I noticed this work of art before?
I pass it every day as I walk out the door.
Look at the expressions on the children's faces,
I never noticed God's gift in this world's fast pace.
Why haven't I told her that I love her?
Instead of thinking, she knows there is no other.
Why haven't I looked her right in the face?
To let her know, no one can take her place.
Yes, I have to do this today, before the sun fades away.

I am glad to sit here all alone, to finally get some thoughts
on where my life has gone.
Why haven't I taken my son and let him know
all about the person he has come from?
To be with him and answer every question,
to understand a small boy's dimension.
To let him know at the end of the day
we can communicate, we can laugh,
we can cry, and even that's okay.
Yes, I have to do this today, before the sun fades away.
I must come up with a plan
to take time out, to help my fellow man.
From my brother, to the people I have never met—
another task to do by sunset.

I am glad to sit here all alone,
to finally get some thoughts on where my life has gone.
Why is this all happening today?
What makes this a very special day?
There must be something in the air
to finally make my soul's senses aware.
I see her smiling at me even though she is not there.
She knows my true feelings of this, she is aware.
My son is with me, his hand in mine.
He is saying, "It is okay, Dad.
I know you meant to give me more time."
I see the trees and flowers growing in a row.
The leaves are falling, it is time for me to go.
As if I were momentarily dreaming,
I hear the siren screaming.
I watch my lifeless body as I circle high above,
the paramedic giving me one last shove.
People kneeling, looking at my face,
blank as a white sheet of paper.
My soul leaves toward space.
Yes, this is a special day;
this is the day I must go away.
It is too bad I couldn't finish my list;
it is too bad I had to die, to see what I have missed.

For You

I do this for you, not for me.
Even though this is small, its goal is tall.
Happy at first, then depressed,
I am not with you because of this.
Because what I have done, I must do this.
Fear not, I am not with you.
In thought, you are my life.
Nothing is more important than this.

When I see you, I see myself; nothing is more rewarding.
My function so small, some may laugh.
I have impressed you; will you always remember this?
Hold your head high, we are one.
Smile as you run.

Tomorrow we will be together, even though you can't wait.
When I see you sleeping, it's not too late.
I'll put my hand upon you.
You will know again tomorrow,
I will have to go.

Her Perfect Little World

Born to a perfect world, never had a worry.
Never had a care, Daddy's money was always there.
Protected like a snow globe, perfect inside,
like the figurines that always had a smile.
The glass was there to keep everyone away;
the glass was there so only the rich could play.
If you shake the globe and put it down,
nothing is disarranged, everything is still sound.
The snow will fall, the water will swirl;
everything will be okay for Daddy's little girl.
Never developed an imagination, always played the game.
Keep Daddy happy, and you will never have any of life's pain.

As she grew up in her snow globe world,
her life was arranged, her life was sold.
When Daddy met Mr. Right,
she was wed; she was everything a man liked.
Behind closed doors, the globe was shaken.
The water swirled;
everything was falling apart for Daddy's little girl.
Even though the glass was cracked,
Daddy fixed it; the water held back.

Reaching for her night drawer, she carefully pulled out a rose
given to her by a boy from a long time ago.
A boy with a beautiful imagination,
a boy who filled her heart with fascination.

The boy she couldn't wait to see,
the boy that was meant to be.

He came from the hard-working class.
He wasn't polished; he didn't shine, like mother's rainbow glass.
He was firstborn generation,
to the parents of dreams and immigration.
He didn't fit in her perfect little world.
Being Daddy's good girl, she sent him away.
She thinks of him every day.
Holding the rose tightly and then letting it fall, she shuts the drawer,
sending the rose back, to before.
Back to the present, back to her perfect world.
Back to her life protected by glass;
back to the world of another class.

The Bitch (Life)

She stares deep into his eyes;
he looks up at her and smiles.
She puts her hand upon his head;
she did not hear a word he said.
She runs her fingers through his hair;
he is hoping this is not just another affair.

Without any further hesitation,
he wants the answer to his question.
She sighs and falls back into the chair;
she plays with the ends of her long red hair.
She smiles to herself, knowing it is her game.
She feels like a rock star at the height of one's fame.

He takes his index fingers, puts them in the corners of
    his eyes.
He refuses to let her see him cry.
Thinking back to the day they met
on the boardwalk close to sunset.
She started in conversation and asked for the first date;
that is what led him to his present fate.
He removes his index fingers and gives her a blank stare;
she is wearing a smile, still playing with her hair.

She is a thunderstorm, distant and out of sight,
but moving closer throughout the night.
She licks her lips and winks her eye.
The love is one way she knows he will never say goodbye.

A Photograph of You

Eyes sparkle, they almost wink;
it makes me wonder what you think.
You lie there in so perfect a pose—
so attractive, so natural, now I know.
Separated by time and place,
the emotions so visible upon your face.
The first could never be the last, your warm embrace.
The womanhood apparent comes focusing through.
The camera only knows what is true.
Like a poet, it reads the lines;
they speak to me, as if your mind.
Soon to meet at that time and place,
soon for me to kiss your face.
Your eyes call me, your smile is true.
Circumstances, more common than we originally knew.
A piece of time has captured your soul;
the image you gave me is now for me to hold.

One Summer, I Met an Angel (A Song)

One summer, I met an angel
One summer, you took my will
More than love is what I left with you
More than love, my life stood still
Our story was a watercolor picture, caught in the rain
The sand running through our fingers, neither was to blame
I have been going places and winding up where I have already been
More than love is what you left me
More than love, the world stood still

The watercolor picture left puddles of bright rain
Dried by the sun's penetrating rays
The colors of a rainbow stirred to a swirl
Our emotions regrouping, creating a new world
More than love is what I left you
More than love, our lives stood still

One summer, I met an angel
One summer, you took my will
One summer, my life was happy
More than love, the world stood still
My patience and harmony are yours to own
Your obligations for me to know
More than love is what you left me

One summer, I met an angel
One summer, you took my will
My world will never be the same without you
The watercolors would wash away
The sun's rays wouldn't deliver a picture
My life would fade away
More than love is what you left me
More than love, my world stood still

Sometimes (A Song)

Sometimes the snow turns to water
Sometimes the rain does freeze
Sometimes the sky is too cloudy
Sometimes for indefinite I can see
The more you love me, the stronger I will be
The more you love me, the further I can see

Sometimes I see your picture
Sometimes I wish you were here with me
Sometimes I think about you
Sometimes I am confused about what is real
The more you love me, the stronger I will be
The more you love me, the further I can see

Sometimes I can't see tomorrow
It's a torment dancing inside of me
Sometimes, sometimes, this is all I can be
Sometimes I stare in your eyes
Sometimes I see what is reflecting at me
Sometimes, sometimes, this is all you can give me

Sometimes the sun turns to darkness
Sometimes the rain does freeze
Sometimes I walk along with you
Sometimes I talk to you through a breeze
The more you love me, the stronger I will be
The more you love me, the further I can see

So, I say to you, my darling
Every day will be a challenge to me
So, I say to you, my darling
It's a torment dancing inside of me
Sometimes, sometimes, this is all I can be
Sometimes I stare in your eyes
Sometimes I see what is reflecting at me
Sometimes, sometimes, this is all you can give me

A Woman Off to War (A Song)

You were standing there
with your short blond hair.
That smile, oh that twinkle in your smile.
You had a grip on me, can't you see
that I just couldn't let you walk by.
I called you that day to hear you say,
"I'll stop and meet you for a while."
I kissed your hand that night,
and you held me tight;
the world stopped passing by.
Like the new day's sun,
something special has just begun.
And now you are going away—
so far, far, away.
It is a year that we will be apart.
You know, you are breaking my heart.
I know this is something you must do;
you know I will wait here for you.

When I see you there,
I want to run my fingers through your hair.
I just want to make love to you.
I think of my life, and I cry at night,
but time you cannot undo.
The time we share together,
my life cannot get any better.
For this, I thank you.

Whether you want to see me when you return
or I am a memory for you to think back,
I will always adore you.
Now this is a special time;
you know you are always on my mind.
I just want to be with you.

And now you are going away—
so far, far, away.
It is a year we will be apart.
You know, you are breaking my heart.
I know this is something you must do.
You know I will wait here for you.

ABOUT THE AUTHOR

Peter Rompf was born in Port Jefferson, New York. He graduated from Sachem High School in Long Island, New York. He joined the US Army and served twenty-two honorable years. He was stationed at Fort Leonard Wood Missouri, Fort Stewart Georgia, Dexheim Germany, has had duty in Iraq, Kuwait, Saudi Arabia, and Fort Hamilton Brooklyn, during September 11, 2001.

After his retirement from the Army, Rompf was an Army JROTC Instructor at Francis Lewis High School, Fresh Meadows, Queens, New York. He coached his JROTC Raider team to nine national championships and then endured his second retirement.

Peter is accredited with a bachelor's degree of science in history from Excelsior College in Albany, New York. He currently lives in Syracuse, New York, with his wife, two children, and two grandchildren.

His hobbies are writing, spending time in nature, photography, riding his Harley-Davidson, spending time with animals, restoring old items, and telling stories of time travel. He is currently working on two novels to be published in the near future.